Let Us Exalt His Name!

A FAMILY ADVENT DEVOTIONAL

Let Us Exalt His Name!

KATIE NETTLES

EDITED BY JOY LA PRADE

SIMPLE FAMILY FAITH
SIMPLEFAMILYFAITH.ORG

Printed in the United States of America.
First Printing, 2018.

ISBN-13 978-0-9980298-0-1 (Paperback)
ISBN-13 978-0-9980298-1-8 (Hardback)
ISBN-13 978-0-9980298-2-5 (Kindle)
ISBN-13 978-0-9980298-3-2 (ePub)

Edited by Joy La Prade.
Cover design by Kirk Brown.
Book Layout by D. Brian Nettles.

Simple Family Faith
https://www.simplefamilyfaith.org

ACKNOWLEDGEMENTS

I am grateful for loving influencers who encouraged me when I needed it most at the beginning. Thanks to Katie, Leah, and my parents. This book exists because of you.

I am thankful to insightful friends who helped me along the way. Thanks to Cathy, Valerie, Alex, Aaron, Pastor Ben, and Pastor Brian. This book is better because of you.

I am gratefully humbled by perceptive collaborators who sacrificially gave of themselves to make this book happen in the end. Thanks to my wise editor Joy La Prade and my creative graphic artist Kirk Brown. This book is available to the world because of you.

Brian Nettles, thank you for being there for every step along the way. His grace and yours has made it all possible.

NOW TO HIM WHO IS ABLE TO KEEP YOU FROM STUMBLING AND TO PRESENT YOU BLAMELESS BEFORE THE PRESENCE OF HIS GLORY WITH GREAT JOY, TO THE ONLY GOD, OUR SAVIOR, THROUGH JESUS CHRIST OUR LORD, BE GLORY, MAJESTY, DOMINION, AND AUTHORITY, BEFORE ALL TIME AND NOW AND FOREVER. AMEN.

JUDE 24-25

For God's glory and my children's joy.

Let Us Exalt His Name!

TABLE OF CONTENTS

Parents' Page

One Advent I realized I longed for my three children to marvel in awe at Jesus. Valuing Jesus in this way is the first step to saving faith and part of a faithful life. So, I prayerfully wrote this book to be a tool that could, by God's grace, cultivate "awe for Jesus."

Setting aside time for family faith-building around holidays is God's original idea. It was His idea to create celebrations that encourage worship and simultaneously create tangible moments to inspire faith in children.

"And when your children say to you, 'What do you mean by this service?' you shall say, 'It is the sacrifice of the LORD's Passover, for he passed over the houses of the people of Israel in Egypt, when he struck the Egyptians but spared our houses.' And the people bowed their heads and worshiped." Exodus 12:26-27

This book is simply a tool for your family to echo the faithfulness of thousands of generations who, at God's prompting, took holidays as pauses in the year's busyness to worship Him and share His story with their children. As a tool, this book can be used as it fits your family.

LET THIS ADVENT DEVOTIONAL FIT YOUR TIME

If your family has time to focus only the last week of advent, then read three devotionals each night while your kids enjoy hot chocolate and crafts (like the ornaments you can download at www.simplefamilyfaith.org) or decorating.

If your family likes to dwell on topics, stretch out this devotional so that Jesus' birthday is read on Christmas and use the time after Christmas to finish the devotionals.

If your family likes to do just a little bit every day, bedtime or breakfast might be a perfect time from December 1st through 25th to finish it all.

LET THIS ADVENT DEVOTIONAL FIT YOUR CHILDREN

If you have a squirmy toddler in your family, you might read while the family eats dessert, makes a nativity with playdough, or plays with blocks on the floor. You might be surprised how much everyone actually learns.

If you have tweens or teens, let them get invested by reading the verses and questions, asking an additional challenging question, leading a prayer or song, or making an accompanying dessert. You can also let them offer additional insight by simply stating "Tell me your thoughts on this."

This book is a simple tool to help you lead your family to grow in awe of our Savior this Advent season. So, use the tool in a way that will bring your family through the Advent season with more awe for our Savior than when they began. If you do that, your family will truly have said with your days, "Let Us Exalt His Name," together.

All unreferenced Scripture can be found at the back of the book.

Introduction

What comes to your mind when you think of God?

What you think about God will change the way you think, the way you act, the way you experience life, and the way you experience eternity. Really, what you think about God is that important.

So, what should we think of when we think about God?

Well, good thing He told us! God tells us about Himself in words that He breathed to faithful, godly men. Those men wrote down each word very carefully. These words from God to people were collected and put in one book—the Bible.

One way God tells us what He is like in the Bible is through giving himself all sorts of different names, like nicknames. God calls Himself Creator because He wants us to know and think of Him as the One who created everything.

Another way God tells us what He is like in the Bible is by stating it directly, like when He said in Deuteronomy, chapter six, "The LORD our God, the LORD is one." From that verse, we understand that there is only one God. He is unique and the only God anywhere.

God is sometimes more indirect and uses stories. These require more careful reading to understand correctly. When God's Son, Jesus, was baptized, God showed that even though there is one God, He is in three persons (God the Father, God the Son, and God the Holy Spirit).* For humans, being one and three at the same time is impossible. But, God is God and things are possible for Him that are beyond our understanding.

When things are beyond our understanding no matter how hard we try to understand them, we have two choices. Our first choice is to stop believing God because we cannot squeeze a God bigger than the universe into the way our brain thinks. Our second choice is to believe God in a special way—through faith and with awe.

Awe is respect stirred together with wonder that bubbles up into our hearts as faith. What is the most beautiful thing you have seen in nature? Awe is the feeling you might get looking at nature and feeling just happy to stand there and marvel at it. Faith is being sure of God—trusting Him—even if you cannot see and understand every detail of Him and His plan, yet.

WHAT we think of God is wrapped up in HOW we think of God. This book will tell a lot of "whats" about God through stories and names and verses. This book has the potential to change "how" you think about God, too. This is not because this book is amazing, but because it is pointing to the One who is the most amazing.

God is the One who can change what and how you think. If you do think of God with faith and awe, your life will exalt (lift up high). His name and that will change the way you think, the way you act, the way you experience life, and the way you experience eternity. Yes, it is that important.

If you would like to, see if you can find the three persons of God (God the Father, God the Son, and God the Holy Spirit) in the story of Jesus' baptism in Matthew 3:16-17.

Jesus is the Creator

**FOR BY HIM [JESUS] ALL THINGS WERE CREATED,
IN HEAVEN AND ON EARTH.
COLOSSIANS 1:16**

"CREATOR" MEANS THE ONE WHO MADE EVERYTHING.

It was completely quiet. Then, a voice like a mighty waterfall filled the emptiness: "Let there be..." God's words started it all. Words created the universe. God needed nothing to make everything. He said, "Let there be" light, darkness, heaven, earth, water, land, plants, animals, and people, and they appeared. And He said they are good!

God created everything except Himself. God is not created; He is the Creator. God has always been and always will be. God is eternal, which means without beginning and without end. This is hard to imagine. But when our imaginations fall short, wonder and amazement for God rush in to fill the place. When you think, "Wow, isn't God amazing?" you are worshiping Him with awe—wonder mixed with respect that comes up as faith in our hearts. The more you think big thoughts of God, the more you worship Him. The more you worship God, the more you see His invisible presence everywhere.

And guess what? There is another amazing thing for us to know about this Creator God. The Bible tells us in Colossians, chapter one, it says this that all things were created by Jesus, and for Jesus.

Another name for Jesus is CREATOR! Jesus did not begin in Bethlehem as a baby. Jesus has always been, even before Bethlehem. Jesus was at Creation because He created it!

Have you ever yelled in triumph, "First!" in a race? Well, Jesus, along with God the Father and God the Spirit could say, "I was first!" or even, "I have always been!"

The next Bible verse says, "By him all things hold together." He does not need ropes to tie the grass to the ground or glue to keep the lion's mane on his head. How does Jesus do that? Only He knows, but isn't it wonderful? Doesn't it fill you with awe as you think, "wow, impressive"? By God the Son's power, everything—from the tallest mountains to a grain of sand—holds together every second of every day. Without Creator Jesus, everything in creation would simply fall apart.

▃▃ ▃▃ ▃▃

GOD THE FATHER, GOD THE SON AND GOD THE SPIRIT ("US") CREATE THE UNIVERSE AND PEOPLE. GENESIS 1:1, 26

WHAT ARE YOU THANKFUL THAT JESUS HOLDS TOGETHER?

IF JESUS HOLDS ALL THINGS TOGETHER, WHAT MIGHT YOU THINK OR FEEL WHEN THINGS SEEM TO BE FALLING APART?

Jesus is the Savior

**THE FATHER HAS SENT HIS SON
TO BE THE SAVIOR OF THE WORLD.
1 JOHN 4:14B**

**A SAVIOR IS ONE WHO RESCUES FROM
RUIN OR DEATH.**

Adam and Eve were the first people God created. Unlike the rest of creation, God formed Adam and Eve a bit like Himself with expressive words, creative ideas, and eternal souls that could be with Him forever. God calls this being made in His image. Adam and Eve lived in a perfect place called the Garden of Eden. They were to take care of the garden.

Having a choice over which tree to pick dinner from was fun. Creating pretty garden paths was a blast. Yet,

the best times were when God came to them in the cool of the day. They felt loved, happy, and free. God had only one simple rule—not to eat of one particular tree. Without worry, pain, or sickness, life was comfortable and joyful. The plants were bursting with food and flowers. The animals bounded up the moment Adam called. Life with God in the Garden of Eden was perfect.

One day things changed. An evil creature named Satan slithered into the garden looking like a snake. He tempted Eve with lies about God. He said God was a liar and that God kept good things from Adam and Eve. With just a few words, Satan captured their minds and hearts. They believed the lies of a created snake over the truth of their Creator God.

When people sin, they think or act as if they know better than God. When people sin, they tell God they do not trust Him or believe that He loves them. Adam and Eve sinned. What looked like just a bite of fruit was really a heart against God. As they crushed the fruit with their teeth, sin crushed their relationship with God.

Have you ever worked hard and created something amazing? How would you feel if someone demolished it and then covered it in black paint? God can understand this. All of creation—beautiful stars, mountains, beaches, lions, flowers, and people— are His work. With Adam and Eve's bite, sin came into God's creation and began to wreck it.

Sin made things worse, bit by bit. The lions did not come when called. The bushes barely had a flower. Adam and Eve hid and began to feel fear, pain, and shame. Worst of all, they could no longer feel God's love, joy, and freedom. Adam and Eve needed a Savior to rescue them from their ruined relationship with God and their ruined life.

God knew the best thing for His people was a close relationship with His care, His comfort, His provision, His joy, and, well, Him. They would never be truly happy, truly themselves, without Him. All people need rescue from sin's ruin. People need a Savior. God promised Adam and Eve He would send a Savior that would crush the snake's head and so crush all sin, too.

Jesus is the promised Savior; the only one who can take away the sin that stains creation and demolishes our relationship with God. When someone believes Jesus, Jesus takes away their sin, and God the Father will be close to them again. Jesus is the only one who can get sinful people and holy God back together. Jesus is the one who can rescue us from ruin. Jesus is the Savior.

AFTER SINNING, ADAM AND EVE DID NOT GO TO GOD, BUT GOD CAME TO THEM.
GENESIS 3:8

WHAT LIES DID SATAN TELL ADAM AND EVE?

WHAT LIES DO KIDS TELL THEMSELVES ABOUT GOD WHEN THEY DISOBEY HIM?

9

Jesus is the Author and Perfecter of Faith

**FIXING OUR EYES ON JESUS, THE AUTHOR
AND PERFECTER OF FAITH
HEBREWS 12:2A (NASB)**

AN AUTHOR DESIGNS OR CREATES SOMETHING AND A PERFECTER MAKES IT PERFECT.

What do you love to do with your family at Christmas? How does your family spend Sundays? Family traditions are important! Adam and Eve had a family tradition, but it shifted from walking with God in the Garden of Eden to running away in sin. Adam and Eve's tradition of not trusting or obeying God continues today with all people on earth. But one person is different. He is fully man and at the same time fully God, and His name is Jesus.

How Jesus can be completely God and completely man at the same time is one of those incredible thoughts that stirs up awe in our hearts. Awe is that mixture of respect and wonder that bubbles up into faith! Faith helps us know that God is much greater than our minds can imagine. This is wonderful. It means God can love, help, direct, and forgive in ways that are bigger than we can understand too!

Adam and Eve's grandchildren and great-grandchildren didn't think big, amazing thoughts about God. Instead, they mostly sinned—thought and acted as if they knew better than God. Those old lies of Satan were stuck like muck inside their heads. God's people needed a Savior, and God was ready to continue the plan.

God had a special friend who trusted Him. This friend had awe for God and faith in God. God would use this man's family to bless the whole world. In fact, Jesus would be sent to grow up in his family! This man's name was Abraham.

God gave this special promise to Abraham in Genesis, chapter twelve, "in you all the families of the earth shall be blessed." Even though Abraham was very old and had no children yet, Abraham believed God's promise that he would have as many great, great, great-grandchildren as there were stars in the sky! God kept His promise to bless all the families of the earth through Abraham when He gave Abraham his great- (41 greats to be exact) grandchild, Jesus!

Jesus is called the "author and perfecter of faith." An author creates a story and a perfecter makes something perfect. Jesus is the one who both starts our faith and grows our faith. Jesus helps us see and know how great God is so we can be sure of Him. Just like a book starts with an author, our faith starts with Jesus because He focuses our mind on God.

Jesus is also the perfecter of our faith. He causes it to bloom. Like a gentle rain, Jesus brings love to our hearts and thinking-what-God-is-like thoughts to our mind. That makes our faith, our being sure of God, grow and grow until it will be perfect one day in heaven. Jesus is the author and perfecter of our faith!

OUR PROMISE-KEEPING GOD MAKES A PROMISE TO ABRAHAM. GENESIS 12:3

WHO IN ABRAHAM'S FAMILY WOULD ONE DAY BLESS ALL THE FAMILIES OF THE EARTH?

WHAT ARE SOME WAYS JESUS IS PERFECTING YOUR FAITH OR THE FAITH OF SOMEONE AROUND YOU?

Jesus is the Deliverer

JESUS WHO DELIVERS US
FROM THE WRATH TO COME.
1 THESSALONIANS 1:10B

A DELIVERER IS ONE WHO BRINGS PEOPLE
OUT OF DANGER INTO SAFETY.

Have you ever looked at the stars at night? In the city you might only see a few. Way out in the countryside you can see what seems like millions and billions of stars. Abraham is well on his way to having that many children in his family! One of his great-grandchildren was Joseph. You may have heard about him because he loved to wear a colorful coat his dad gave him. He had that coat because his dad liked Joseph best of all his sons.

God gave Joseph many great ideas, often in dreams. Joseph's brothers were tired of their father's favorite son and his dreams, so they sold him as a slave to people traveling to Egypt. Joseph had a hard time in Egypt, but God protected him. He made Joseph smart and gave him the ability to understand what dreams meant. Before long, Joseph was right beside the king, Pharaoh, helping lead the whole country! His brothers did not think that would happen!

12

But famine was on its way to everyone in and around Egypt. Famine means the ground would not grow food people needed. Hunger reached far and wide, even all the way up to Joseph's family! They headed to Egypt to buy food from the only person who had it. They had no idea it was going to be their brother!

God gave Joseph good ideas to prepare for the famine. He had everyone in Egypt store up food before the famine began. Joseph's brothers got a shock to see the brother they had sold as a slave helping to lead Egypt! They pleaded with Joseph for forgiveness. God helped Joseph see something big: what his brothers meant for evil, God meant for good, to help all of Abraham's family have food to survive. Before long, the whole family moved to be with Joseph in Egypt!

With God's help, Joseph delivered his family and many others from starving to death. God used Joseph to save Abraham's family and keep His promise to Abraham: "in you all the families of the earth shall be blessed." Jesus would be not just a family member, but the Deliverer, too.

Jesus would one day deliver all the families of the earth from a hunger for relationship with God. Joseph delivered his family from starving to death. Jesus can deliver us from a forever death separated from God. Then, we can be safe with God forever in heaven, filled with God's love, happiness, and freedom.

But why does Jesus need to deliver us? God has the right to be angry about our sin. Jesus accepted God's anger and punishment (God's wrath) for our sin on the cross. Jesus delivered us from the punishment we deserve from God by taking the punishment on Himself. Wow, isn't that amazing? Jesus delivers peace and a forever life close to God (in heaven) to all who have faith in Him. Jesus is our Deliverer.

**JOSEPH TELLS HIS BROTHERS HOW HE FELT.
GENESIS 50:19-20**

THINGS LIKE PIZZA, MAIL, AND PACKAGES ARE DELIVERED EVERY DAY. JESUS IS A MUCH MORE IMPORTANT, ETERNAL DELIVERER. WHAT DOES JESUS DELIVER TO US?

IF GOD COULD CHANGE THE BAD THINGS THAT HAPPENED TO JOSEPH INTO GOOD, HOW COULD WE THINK OR FEEL DIFFERENTLY ABOUT BAD THINGS WHEN THEY COME?

Jesus is the Lamb of God

**BEHOLD, THE LAMB OF GOD,
WHO TAKES AWAY THE SIN OF THE WORLD!
JOHN 1:29B**

**THE LAMB OF GOD IS A NAME FOR THE PERFECT
PERSON WHO TAKES THE PUNISHMENT WE DESERVE
FOR SIN.**

Have you ever noticed one kid will bully and be mean to another kid just to keep some power? Abraham's family, who were called the Israelites, were bullied in Egypt for 400 years. The new Pharaoh forgot Joseph but remembered the huge numbers of Israelites. Pharaoh was afraid they might try to take over, so he forced Abraham's family to be slaves. They worked all day making muddy bricks and hauling big stones. Some Israelites cried out in prayer to God. God still loved them and His plan to rescue them was still on time.

One day an Egyptian princess wanted to bring a little Israelite baby boy home to live with her, but he was too young to be separated from his mother. So this baby boy, Moses, spent years listening to his mother talk and sing about God and Abraham before he moved to the palace. God positioned Moses perfectly in both families so he could help rescue Abraham's family, called the Israelites, from slavery.

God spoke to Moses and instructed him to tell Pharaoh, "Let my people

14

go!" Pharaoh answered, "No!" So, God sent terrible things called plagues. Each plague matched a fake god of the Egyptians to prove God's truth and power over those fake gods. The water turned into blood, the frogs hopped in by the thousands, flies buzzed by the millions, sores oozed by the billions! But the bully Pharaoh refused to admit God's ultimate power!

While the Egyptians suffered, God kept His people safe from the plagues, but the worst plague was coming. Abraham's family had to prepare. Each family had to kill a lamb right before the dark of night. They were to put the lamb's blood on the tops and sides of their wooden door frames to show they believed God.

That night at midnight God came into Egypt. The door frames not stained in lamb's blood were doors God entered and killed the firstborn child of the family. This night is still remembered among the Israelites. It is called the Passover because God passed over the families who put blood on their doorposts.

Crying filled the night as people woke up to death. The Egyptians trembled with fear, so Moses led the Israelites out of Egypt. The Egyptians were so happy the Israelites were going, they gave them gold and silver and treasure to take with them. The Israelites saw that God has more power than any bully. Awe for God and faith in Him grew in their hearts.

Jesus is called the "Lamb of God." He was killed just like the Passover lamb. His blood stained not a wooden door frame, but a wooden cross. The Passover lamb's blood kept people's bodies alive. The Lamb of God's blood keeps people's souls alive.

Jesus is an even better and more perfect sacrifice than the Passover lamb. His blood does not prevent just one night of God's judgment. Jesus' sacrifice takes away sin to prevent God's forever judgment. He is our truer and better Passover lamb. He is the Lamb of God.

ᴧᴧ ᴧᴧ ᴧᴧ

GOD EXPLAINS THE NIGHT OF PASSOVER.
EXODUS 12:12-14

WHY IS THE NAME "LAMB OF GOD" A GOOD NAME FOR JESUS?

WHAT FEELINGS AND THOUGHTS DO YOU HAVE ABOUT JESUS BEING YOUR LAMB OF GOD?

15

Jesus is the One Who Sets Us Free

SO IF THE SON SETS YOU FREE,
YOU WILL BE FREE INDEED.
JOHN 8:36

"THE ONE WHO SETS US FREE" IS THE PERSON WHO FREES US FROM SIN AND THE EFFECTS OF SIN.

Have you ever told a lie and then felt trapped? If you admitted you told the lie, you might get in trouble. It felt like you had to keep lying to protect the one lie. Sin always seems to trap us. But God wants us to enjoy His freedom. Jesus coming to set us free was always God's perfect plan from the beginning. God was not surprised by Adam and Eve's sin or Pharaoh's hard heart.

Yet, Pharaoh was surely shocked by God's power. That bully Pharaoh thought he was bigger and stronger than God, until God showed Pharaoh that He controlled even the breath of his firstborn son. Pharaoh finally realized just how powerful the one true God was, so he let God's people go.

Millions of Israelite feet walked out of Egypt that day. Moses followed God's direction and led all the boys, girls, men, and women of Abraham's family toward a great sea.

But it was not long before Pharaoh's fear was washed away by a wave of anger that all his slaves were gone. Pharaoh and his soldiers got their horses and chariots and chased after the Israelites. God's people could not possibly fight him and win. They were trapped, with the sea in front of them and their enemies behind them.

Moses told the scared Israelites, "Fear not, stand firm, and see the salvation of the Lord, which he will work for you today... The Lord will fight for you, and you have only to be silent." That night God blocked Pharaoh and his men from moving forward. And then God blew back the waters of the sea. The breath that spoke all creation into existence had no trouble blowing back the waters of the sea until there was dry land.

Now, all those feet that had just walked out of Egypt made footprints on the bottom of the sea. Abraham's family walked to safety while staying dry. When Pharaoh and his men tried to chase the Israelites, God allowed the sea to rush back over them. They all died.

After 400 years of slavery, the Israelites had escaped their slave master, Pharaoh. They would never have to make another brick or move a single stone for him again. They sang songs of praise to God. God had set them free!

Jesus sets us free from slavery to sin. Sin ties us down with lies that God doesn't really love us. Sin captures our joy and freedom with the lies that we don't need to listen to God and that we'll be happier without Him. If we believe one sinful lie, soon we will hear a new lie that sounds good to follow. It seems like we cannot escape the endless work of trying to be happy in sin. So, we are slaves to sin.

Not only does Jesus set our minds free from the chains of sinful ideas, but He sets our souls free from the ultimate effect of sin. Sin always locks us up far from the one true, loving God. When we believe in Jesus, He breaks the slavery to sin that keeps us trapped. With those chains gone, we burst into song celebrating our escape and the one who freed us. When Jesus frees us, we are truly free. He fills us with peace and love. Jesus is the One who sets us free.

MOSES AND THE PEOPLE CELEBRATE WITH A PRAISE SONG TO GOD. EXODUS 15:1-2

WHAT DOES JESUS SET US FREE FROM?

WHO IS TRULY FREE: SOMEONE WHO BELIEVES IN JESUS WHO IS IN JAIL OR SOMEONE TAKING A WALK IN YOUR NEIGHBORHOOD WHO DOES NOT BELIEVE IN JESUS?

Jesus is the Bread of Life

JESUS SAID TO THEM, "I AM THE BREAD OF LIFE; WHOEVER
COMES TO ME SHALL NOT HUNGER."
JOHN 6:35A

**THE "BREAD OF LIFE" IS A PERSON WHO COMPLETELY
SATISFIES OUR SPIRITUAL HUNGER.**

If you were going camping for a while, what would be the most important things to take along? After God brought the Israelites out of Egypt, He sent them camping for about forty years! He didn't send them to a sheltered area by a river with fields of berries. God sent them to a desert. There was no food there.

Why would God lead His people to where they couldn't find food for themselves? God wanted them to know He could be trusted to care for them. The Israelites should have already learned this lesson. But even after seeing God's awe-inspiring power when He saved them at the Passover and the Sea, they seemed to forget God's goodness and greatness in the blink of an eye.

In the desert, the Israelites got hungry and quickly complained. God heard them. He decided to give the Israelites bread each day, so they could

18

rely on Him. The next morning, they woke up to see flakes of something all over the ground. The people were so surprised! "What is it?" they asked. It was manna, a sweet flake-like bread from heaven.

Now they did not have to work hard for their food by planting seeds, weeding the gardens, harvesting the crop, grinding the grain, kneading the dough, or baking the bread. All they had to do was gather it! It was the perfect gift of God for people "on the go" in a desert land. God provided in one food all the things their bodies needed for life and health, and it tasted sweet too!

Jesus is called the "Bread of Life." The bread in the desert provided a way for God's people to survive physically. Jesus provides a way for God's people to live spiritually. When we trust Jesus, He softly, invisibly fills up our hearts with Himself. Then we will be fulfilled and happy because we will be close to God now on earth and we will be close to God one day in heaven forever.

Like the bread in the desert, our "Bread of Life" is sweet, filling, and all we need! We do not have to work to fill our hungry hearts. Jesus gives Himself freely to us so we can learn to be sure of Him.

When your heart feels hungry with loneliness, Jesus can fill it with His friendship. When your heart feels hungry with sadness, Jesus can fill it with His joy. When your heart feels hungry with fear, Jesus can fill it with His peace. Jesus is our true Bread of Life.

THIS IS WHAT IT WAS LIKE THE FIRST TIME MANNA APPEARED. EXODUS 16:14-15

MANNA WAS THE ISRAELITES' MAIN FOOD FOR A LONG, LONG TIME. THEY WERE AMAZED BY THE MIRACLE OF MANNA AT FIRST, BUT BEFORE TOO LONG, IT DIDN'T SEEM LIKE A BIG DEAL ANYMORE. WHAT ARE SOME WAYS GOD HAS PROVIDED FOR YOU OR YOUR FAMILY THAT ARE A BIG DEAL (THAT YOU MIGHT NOT REALLY NOTICE ANYMORE)?

WHEN YOUR HEART FEELS HUNGRY FOR SOMETHING, WHAT DO YOU THINK ABOUT JESUS CALLING HIMSELF THE BREAD OF LIFE?

19

Jesus is our Judge

AND HE COMMANDED US TO PREACH TO THE PEOPLE AND TO TESTIFY THAT HE [JESUS] IS THE ONE APPOINTED BY GOD TO BE JUDGE OF THE LIVING AND THE DEAD.
ACTS 10:42

A JUDGE IS A PERSON WHO HAS THE AUTHORITY TO OBSERVE AND DECIDE WHAT IS RIGHT AND WRONG.

After their time in the desert, God led the Israelites to the land He had promised Abraham long ago. He wanted them to build houses and enjoy this Promised Land. It was such a nice place to live. Bees could make buckets and buckets of honey visiting all the flowers. The cows had plenty of grass to eat, so they could give gallons and gallons of milk. It was a land flowing with milk and honey!

Before the Israelites settled in, God told them to clean up. He told them to make sure all the other people in this Promised Land leave, because they worshiped fake gods. The people believed that these fake gods, called idols, would give them what they wanted. Does this sound like a familiar lie? Sin tells us we don't need God and we can be happy without Him. Trusting anything besides the God of the Bible to save us is called idolatry.

But the Israelites didn't do the one thing God said. Instead of cleaning the evil people out of the land, the Israelites let them stay. Eventually, they decided to marry them! Soon, they were even trusting in the fake gods!

God loves His people too much to leave them alone in their sin. Before long the Israelites were suffering attacks from other countries. They prayed to God for help. His loving response was to send judges to free His people from their enemies.

God sent many different judges to help free His people. God gave Samson amazing muscles and strength to free God's people. God gave Gideon great ideas and courage to free God's people. God gave Deborah wisdom and insight to free God's people. Each time, the judge followed God's plan and the Israelites could live in peace. Each time God set them free, the

Israelites eventually felt they no longer needed Him and turned back to their idols. Again, enemies would attack and Israel would pray and God would send a judge to bring peace. Do you see a pattern?

Jesus is called our "Judge" because He knows what is right and wrong and has the power, position, and authority to give His enemies the punishment they deserve for their sin. The judges in the Promised Land would free God's people from God's enemies for a time. Jesus frees us from the enemy of sin forever. Samson had some strength, Gideon had a few ideas, Deborah had limited wisdom, but Jesus has all strength, all knowledge, and all wisdom. No enemy will ever stand against our Judge Jesus and win. Jesus is the best and truest Judge.

♛ ♛ ♛

**THIS VERSE SHOWS WHAT HAPPENED WHEN THE ISRAELITES DID NOT CLEAN UP THE PROMISED LAND.
JUDGES 2:12**

WHAT WAS THE PATTERN OF THE ISRAELITES DURING THE TIME OF JUDGES?

GOD SAW THE ISRAELITES' PATTERN OF BEHAVIOR YET KEPT HELPING. WHAT DOES THAT SAY ABOUT GOD?

Jesus is
King of Kings and
Lord of lords

**A KING IS A LEADER AND COMMANDER OF THE
PEOPLE IN HIS LAND. A LORD IS THE MASTER WHO
HAS THE POWER TO DECIDE FOR HIS PEOPLE.**

The last judge in Israel was Samuel, and God used him in mighty ways to deliver the Israelites from their enemies. Samuel was getting old. The Israelites wondered—who would lead them now? The kings of other countries seemed easy to follow. You could see them and hear them. When other kings would shout out laws from their palaces, Israel's God and King would whisper to the hearts of His people. God knew this whispering could help the Israelites lean in and stay close to Him, where they could be safe and know His love.

But the Israelites wanted the shouts of a man instead of the whispers of God. They asked Samuel to find a human king. God said to Samuel, "Obey the voice of the people in all that they say to you, for they have not rejected you, but they have rejected me from being king over them."

So, some good kings ruled and some bad kings ruled, but none of them could be as good of a king as God. The bad kings led the people to worship idols. They trusted in those fake gods and turned away from God's protection. Enemies came into the Israelites' land, dividing The Kingdom of Israel in two. They forced some Israelites to leave their homes and live far away in exile. God was not surprised. He already knows everything that has been, is now, and will be. Does that fill you with awe to just think about?

About sixty years after Jesus died on the cross, God allowed one of His followers named John to peek into the future. God showed John how King Jesus would come back to earth one day, to set all things right. Jesus will not come as a baby this time, but as a conquering King wearing a robe that says, "King of kings and Lord of lords." King Jesus is all wise, all knowing, all good, all loving, and all powerful. King Jesus has more power than we can imagine and loves us more completely than we could dream. Unlike other leaders, King Jesus perfectly takes care of His people, perfectly protects His people, and perfectly leads His people.

The Israelites wanted a human king they could see. One day, the Israelites' desire to see the face of their king will come true for all people. One day everyone will see Jesus, and at His name, "every knee should bow, in heaven and on earth and under the earth, and every tongue confess that Jesus Christ is Lord, to the glory of God the Father." One day every president, king, pharaoh, neighbor, friend, man, woman, boy, and girl will bow before King Jesus. What a day that will be! Jesus is the King of kings and Lord of lords.

**READ ABOUT THE PEOPLE REJECTING GOD AS THEIR KING.
1 SAMUEL 8:6-7**

HOW DOES IT MAKE YOU THINK AND FEEL TO KNOW JESUS THE KING OF KINGS HAS MORE POWER THAN ANY TEACHER, COUNTRY, OR GOVERNMENT?

WHAT ARE THINGS WE MIGHT THINK OR DO TO REJECT JESUS AS OUR KING?

Jesus is the Son of David

AND THE CROWDS THAT WENT BEFORE HIM [JESUS] AND THAT FOLLOWED HIM WERE SHOUTING, "HOSANNA TO THE SON OF DAVID! BLESSED IS HE WHO COMES IN THE NAME OF THE LORD! HOSANNA IN THE HIGHEST!"
MATTHEW 21:9

THE SON OF DAVID IS A TITLE FOR JESUS BECAUSE HE IS THE MOST IMPORTANT OF DAVID'S CHILDREN AND GRANDCHILDREN.

Look around you. Do you see anything that will last forever? God promised one of the Kings of Israel something that would last forever. What could it be?

The second king in Israel was David. As a young man he was a shepherd, and he sang songs to God because he loved and trusted in Him. David trusted in God's strength when he protected sheep against lions and bears. When he was a little older, David trusted in God's strength when he fought the giant Goliath and killed him.

Everyone cheered for David's courage that day. God cheered to see his heart. God knew David loved Him and had faith in Him. He chose David to be Israel's king. David made many mistakes and sinned, but he kept trusting that God was good. David would turn to God and tell Him how he felt, even after he had sinned.

24

God made a promise to David, "your house and your kingdom shall be made sure forever before me. Your throne shall be established forever." This meant his children and grandchildren would always rule over Israel. After David died, his son did become king. But before too long, the nation of Israel broke apart. Enemies came into the land and took many of God's people away to other countries in exile. It seemed like Israel was destroyed forever.

What about God's promise to David? God never lies, but He often does things differently from how we think He should. Jesus is called the "Son of David" because He is David's great-grandson (27 greats). Like David, Jesus had a heart that was faithful to lead God's people. The people of Israel saw this and called Jesus the Son of David. They thought He was a king who would lead a battle to defeat their enemies.

Jesus, the Son of David, did come to be a King. But Jesus created His kingdom in the hearts of everyone who trusts in Him. God's promise to David is true because God knew Jesus would come later in David's family. Jesus would have a forever house, a forever kingdom, and a forever throne in heaven and in the hearts of His people.

Jesus came to earth to protect His people in a greater way than defeating one giant. By dying on the cross, He defeated the sin that separated them from God the Father. One day Jesus will come again and show that He is King over all creation! We will see that Jesus' kingdom is greater and more majestic than David's kingdom ever was. Everyone will see Jesus on His forever throne. Jesus is the forever King. Jesus is the Son of David.

♦♦♦ ♦♦♦ ♦♦♦

**HERE GOD MAKES HIS PROMISES TO DAVID.
2 SAMUEL 7:12, 16**

**WHEN GOD PROMISED DAVID A FOREVER KINGDOM,
WHO WOULD BE THE FOREVER KING?**

**GOD FULFILLED HIS PROMISE TO DAVID DIFFERENTLY THAN DAVID
COULD HAVE EXPECTED. HOW MIGHT WE MISS SEEING
GOD'S FULFILLED PROMISES IN OUR LIVES?**

Jesus is the High Priest

SINCE THEN WE HAVE A GREAT HIGH PRIEST WHO HAS PASSED THROUGH THE HEAVENS, JESUS, THE SON OF GOD, LET US HOLD FAST OUR CONFESSION.

HEBREWS 4:14

THE HIGH PRIEST WAS THE SPIRITUAL LEADER OF GOD'S PEOPLE AND MADE SACRIFICES FOR THEIR SINS.

What could you learn about your friends by visiting their houses? People's houses and the things inside them show us something about who they are! This was true about God's house, called the Temple.

God told David's son, King Solomon, to build a house for Him. He gave King Solomon exact instructions about how it should look. God wanted a place where people could come to be near Him and learn about Him. God is not limited by a building—He is everywhere!—but His presence would be in the Temple in a special way.

The Temple was lovely. It had walls covered in gold! It was decorated with jewels and with carvings of flowers and fruit and angels, but God being there was the most beautiful thing about it. There was an important room called the Holy of Holies. This room held the Ark of the Covenant, a big, golden box with precious things inside, like the Ten Commandments. There were two golden angels on top, and the place in between the angels was called the Mercy Seat. God told His people He would meet with them here.

But the Holy of Holies was too special for just anyone to come inside. Only one person who asked God to atone for (cover over) his sin could go into God's special room. This person was the greatest leader in the temple, called the high priest. He could only enter the Holy of Holies once a year! When he came in, he had to bring the blood of an animal that had been killed. He would sprinkle the blood on the Mercy Seat and ask for that to cover over the people's sin.

Jesus did not work at the temple, but He is our great High Priest. He does not need the blood of animals to cover people's sin. His blood that spilled out on the cross when He died does not just cover sin for a little while; it takes away all sin as if it had never been there. The high priest at the temple only went to God once a year to ask Him to forgive His people. Jesus now sits right beside God in heaven and constantly asks God the Father to help those who are trusting in Him. Jesus is our High Priest.

GOD SPEAKS ABOUT THE TEMPLE THAT WAS JUST BUILT.
2 CHRONICLES 7:15-16

WHAT DID JESUS DO TO TAKE AWAY SINS?

WHAT COULD YOU LEARN ABOUT GOD FROM WHAT THE TEMPLE WAS LIKE?

Jesus is the Messiah

THE WOMAN SAID TO HIM, "I KNOW THAT MESSIAH IS COMING (HE WHO IS CALLED CHRIST). WHEN HE COMES, HE WILL TELL US ALL THINGS." JESUS SAID TO HER, "I WHO SPEAK TO YOU AM HE."
JOHN 4:25-26

THE MESSIAH IS THE ONE CHOSEN AND SENT BY GOD TO SAVE GOD'S PEOPLE.

Have you ever had to wait for someone special to show up at your house, like a cousin or an aunt? When they arrive there will be smiles and hugs and maybe a treat. Sometimes it seems like you have to wait forever! The Israelites were promised someone good was coming to them, but they had to wait for Him for hundreds of years.

God promised He would send this leader to His people to save them from their enemies, especially the enemy of sin, so they could be close to God again. The prophets in the Bible spoke a lot about this promised leader. Prophets are people who tell the words of God, and when they speak about the future it is called prophecy.

There were hundreds of very old prophecies about this special leader sent by God, called the Messiah. There was even a prophecy by the prophet Micah that said He would be born in

28

Bethlehem. So, who was this promised one who would bring God's people back to Him? Who would fulfill God's promise to Eve to crush the serpent's head and sin along with it? Who would fulfill God's promise to Abraham to bless all nations? Who would fulfill God's promise to David for a forever kingdom and forever throne?

God sent many words to the prophets for His people. Then there was silence from God for 400 years. Those who read the Scriptures waited and watched. God's people watched as their enemies became strong. They waited for the day they could be close to God again, safe in their own land. When would the Messiah come? In the stillness of the night, they prayed for Him to appear. Their hearts ached for the one they knew they needed. All of Bethlehem watched their little children with questioning eyes.

Jesus is the Messiah. He is the one promised to the Israelites through the prophecies. He is the One prom-ised to Eve, Abraham, and David. He is the promised one sent by God to bring us back to God. His perfect life, sin-crushing death, and God-glorifying resurrection changed the entire history of God's people and creation itself.

One day Jesus will come again to bring His people to heaven, where there will be no more pain, death, or sadness. We who love Jesus now can understand a bit of how God's people felt before Jesus came the first time, because now we wait for Jesus to come again. Today, Jesus has His kingdom in the hearts of His people, but one day He will come with power to make all His creation new again—His perfect, forever kingdom. Can you imagine what that will be like?

Today, we look forward to when He comes again, not as a baby, but as the powerful King of the World. Jesus is our Messiah and we pray for Him to come back soon. Come, Lord Jesus!

▰▰ ▰▰ ▰▰

AN OLD MAN WHO WAITED A LONG TIME FOR THE MESSIAH FIRST SEES HIM. LUKE 2:25-30

WHAT DOES THE NAME MESSIAH MEAN?

HOW DOES JESUS, THE MESSIAH, FULFILL GOD'S PROMISES TO EVE, ABRAHAM, AND DAVID?

Jesus is the Wonderful Counselor, Mighty God, Everlasting Father, Prince of Peace

AND HIS NAME SHALL BE CALLED WONDERFUL COUNSELOR, MIGHTY GOD, EVERLASTING FATHER, PRINCE OF PEACE
ISAIAH 9:6B

What name did Jesus write on His paper at school? There are so many names from which to choose. Would it be Lamb of God, Savior, Deliverer, King of kings and Lord of lords, Messiah, or Son of David?

God has given His people many names for Jesus. He did this so we could learn who He is and how He cares for us. Through Isaiah the prophet, God gave many names all at once!

Prophet Isaiah wrote this in chapter nine of Isaiah many years before Jesus was born.

For to us a child is born,
to us a son is given;
and the government shall be upon his shoulder,
and his name shall be called
Wonderful Counselor, Mighty God, Everlasting Father, Prince of Peace.

Who is the child that is born? Who is the son given to us? God the Son, Jesus, was God's gift to the world that first Christmas. One of the most famous verses in the Bible explains this. John 3:16 declares, "For God so loved the world, that He gave his only begotten Son, that whoever believes in him shall not perish, but have eternal life" (NASB). This child will be so strong He can give eternal life to everyone who believes in Him! He will be so strong that the governments of the whole world will be easily managed on just one shoulder!

When someone believes in Jesus, they have eternal life in Heaven with God. One day, they will be able to walk and talk with Him, just like Adam and Eve did before sin ruined the world. In Heaven, Jesus will be our Wonderful Counselor, Mighty God, Everlasting Father, and Prince of Peace in ways our minds cannot understand, yet.

The good news is Jesus can be these things even now for those who believe in Him. He can be our Wonderful Counselor, filling us with wonder at who God is and giving us wisdom. Even now Jesus can be our Mighty God, rescuing us from our enemy, sin, and giving us strength to follow Him. Even now Jesus can be our Everlasting Father, the one who gives love, guidance, and help. Even now Jesus can be our Prince of Peace, the One who is with us, bringing us peace.

God, help us to believe in Jesus so He can be our Wonderful Counselor, our Mighty God, our Everlasting Father, and our Prince of Peace!

ISAIAH EXPLAINS ALL THAT THE MESSIAH WILL BE TO HIS PEOPLE. ISAIAH 9:6-7

HOW IS JESUS (GOD THE SON) LIKE A GIFT TO US FROM GOD THE FATHER?

WHICH NAME OF JESUS WOULD HELP YOU MOST RIGHT NOW IN YOUR LIFE?

Jesus is Immanuel

**THEY SHALL CALL HIS NAME IMMANUEL
(WHICH MEANS, GOD WITH US).
MATTHEW 1:23B**

IMMANUEL MEANS "GOD WITH US."

Can you imagine what it would have been like to go from the bright presence of God the Father in the beauty and happiness of heaven to being curled up inside the dark of a woman's tummy for months? What would it feel like to be born, and to suddenly have the pain of hunger, the limits of skin, the need for drink, the inability to do anything for yourself when you had created everything?

An angel told a young woman named Mary she was going to have a baby, even though she was not married,

because God's Spirit put the baby inside her. The angel said this baby would be "God with us." Can you imagine the awe of knowing God the Son would be with people in a way they could see and touch? He would be named Jesus and would save His people from their sin. Then an angel told a man named Joseph to take Mary as his wife, adopt Jesus as his child, and to take care of them both.

When Mary was almost ready to have the baby, they had to take a long journey. The government was forcing everyone to go back to their hometowns. Joseph was David's (26 greats) grandchild. Since David was from Bethlehem, that is where they went.

Joseph had to find a private place for Mary to rest, but all the places to stay were full except where the animals stayed. When Jesus was born Joseph and Mary put him in a manger, which normally held hay for animals to eat. They must have wondered, "Why would God's Son be born around animal smells and noises?" Even though they didn't understand everything, Joseph and Mary (unlike Adam and Eve) believed God was true and good. They had faith that His plans were greater than what they could see, and they trusted Him.

Jesus did not glow with heavenly light when He was born. Really, He looked just like other little babies. Mary and Joseph might have had glimpses of God's plan for His son, but so much of their lives would be spent waiting to see it. Meanwhile, they fed Jesus, taught Jesus, and took care of Jesus.

Before Jesus was born, God gave him another name. Every Christmas the world celebrates this name. It is "Immanuel," which means "God with us." Isn't this amazing? How could our holy (above all and perfect) God be with sinful people? In the Temple, the high priest needed to sacrifice many animals before he stepped a toe into God's presence in the Holy of Holies. How could it be possible for humans to walk and talk with God on earth?

This is something we cannot fully understand or explain, but we can be in awe of it. God's ways are not man's ways. In Jesus, God the Son stayed God and yet also became a tiny human that could be held in the arms of a young woman next to a manger in Bethlehem.

God is with us in Jesus. The wonder of that will never end. God the Son came to us in the soft form of a baby. Our awe at God's amazing gift will forever bubble up as faith in the hearts of God's people. Jesus, thank you for being God with us! Jesus is our Immanuel.

HERE IS HOW JESUS WAS BORN.
LUKE 2:6

WHAT DOES THE NAME IMMANUEL MEAN?

WHAT IS HARD TO IMAGINE ABOUT GOD THE SON COMING TO EARTH AS A BABY?

Jesus is The Christ

FOR UNTO YOU IS BORN THIS DAY IN THE CITY OF DAVID
A SAVIOR, WHO IS CHRIST THE LORD.
LUKE 2:11

THE CHRIST IS THE PERSON CHOSEN AND SENT BY GOD TO SAVE GOD'S PEOPLE.

Have you ever noticed how easy it is to slip into doing something wrong, but how hard it sometimes seems to do something right? God says we are all like sheep who wander around and do not listen well. Because we keep running away, it would not be easy for God to complete His plan to bring His people near to Him again. But God promised He would send someone to rescue us and bring us back. He would be a Savior, Christ the Lord.

On the night Jesus was born in Bethlehem, the shepherds out in the fields were the first to hear the news. A bright light appeared in the sky and suddenly there were angels everywhere praising God!

It must have been quite a shock. Then an angel said, "Fear not, for behold, I bring you good news of great joy that will be for all the people. For unto you is born this day in the city of David a Savior, who is Christ the

Lord." Good news of great joy is what God's people needed. That is what Creation needed. This good news was not just for Abraham's children, but for all people—for all families of the earth, just as God promised!

Jesus Christ is the sent Savior, and that is just who we needed to rescue us from our sin. "Christ" means the anointed one. In the Bible, kings were anointed with oil to show they had been chosen to lead. The Christ was chosen by God for God's special job.

After announcing that the Christ had come, the angels gave the shepherds directions to the baby. Well, the shepherds wasted no time and quickly ran to find Jesus. They were amazed to see Him—the Christ had come! They started telling everyone!

When a person believes in Jesus, most people call them a Christian. Do you see the word "Christ" in Christian? That is because as Christians we believe in and try to be like Christ Jesus. Christ Jesus told people about God's plan for the world, just like the shepherds. As Christians, we can be like Jesus and the shepherds and tell the good news of great joy. The news is not just for us! It is for all people. Unto us is born a Savior, Christ the Lord!

▰▰ ▰▰ ▰▰

THIS IS WHAT THE SHEPHERDS SAW AND HEARD THAT NIGHT.
LUKE 2:8-14

CAN YOU THINK OF A WAY TO SHARE THE GOOD NEWS OF GREAT JOY?

WHAT DO YOU THINK IS THE MOST SURPRISING THING THE ANGELS SAID?

Jesus is the Light of the World

AGAIN JESUS SPOKE TO THEM, SAYING, "I AM THE LIGHT OF THE WORLD. WHOEVER FOLLOWS ME WILL NOT WALK IN DARKNESS, BUT WILL HAVE THE LIGHT OF LIFE."
JOHN 8:12

THE LIGHT OF THE WORLD IS THE ONE WHO SHINES BRILLIANTLY AND PURELY TO REVEAL TRUTH AND EVIL.

Has your teacher ever given you a look that made you sit up straight or a friend given you goofy googly eyes that made you laugh? Sometimes, when people want to tell you something, they have to get your attention first. God certainly did this when He sent angels to tell the shepherds about Jesus!

But every once in a while someone will really be paying attention to you. They will see a glimmer in your eye and know what you mean without you even saying a word. The wise men who visited the baby Jesus were these kind of people. They figured out so much, not from a glimmer in God's eye, but from a glimmer in His sky.

These men had really studied the Old Testament Scriptures, so they knew what a new star over Israel would mean. It would mean the birth of the King of the Jews. (The Jews are the Israelites who all came from

Abraham.) The wise men were ready to worship Him and bring gifts worthy of the King.

Like the glimmering star, the gifts said so much about what was happening without saying a word. Gold said the wise men considered Jesus worthy (full of worth and value) and royal. Frankincense was an incense (similar to a perfume) used during temple worship to God. This gift said they saw Jesus as God's Son, the perfect Great High Priest. Myrrh was used when preparing dead bodies to be buried. This was a very strange gift. But since the wise men read the scriptures, they knew this baby would grow up, suffer, and die for the people He loved.

The wise men were guided by a small speck of light through very dark nights. That light led them to Jesus, who is also called the Light of the World. This world and many people in this world are full of darkness because sin still has control. When we believe in Jesus, He becomes our light. He allows us to see what is true about God and helps us recognize the lies of sin. He shows us God's love for us, so that we can trust Him and come near to Him again.

For believers, Jesus' light continues to grow until the day in heaven when we see Him face to face. Then, the light will be fully bright as we know fully and are fully known. If we trust in Jesus, we will never be alone in the dark. He will brighten our lives and He will be our Light of the World.

⚜ ⚜ ⚜

THE WISE MEN WORSHIP JESUS.
MATTHEW 2:1-2, 9-12

IN THE DARK, HOW DO YOU FEEL WITHOUT A LIGHT? HOW MIGHT PEOPLE FEEL WITHOUT JESUS IN THEIR LIVES?

WHAT ARE SOME WAYS THAT HAVING A SPIRITUAL LIGHT IN YOUR LIFE WOULD BE HELPFUL?

Jesus is our Good Shepherd

I AM THE GOOD SHEPHERD. THE GOOD SHEPHERD LAYS
DOWN HIS LIFE FOR THE SHEEP.
JOHN 10:11

**A GOOD SHEPHERD IS A PERSON WHO TAKES GOOD
CARE OF SHEEP.**

What do you know about sheep? Did you know they aren't very good at taking care of themselves? They need someone to help make sure they get food and water and don't wander into danger.

God says we are all like sheep. And many of the leaders God gave His people were shepherds. Abraham had many herds of sheep when God made His promise to him. Before God used Moses to lead His people through the sea and desert, Moses kept sheep too. David took care of sheep before he led Israel as king. Chasing sheep was probably good practice for leading God's people!

When Jesus grew up into a man, He was followed around by large crowds of people. They wanted to hear His teaching and have him heal them. One day, He was out in a boat when He noticed all those people were just standing on the shore waiting for Him to come help. To Jesus, they looked like lost sheep.

"When he went ashore he saw a great crowd, and he had compassion on them, because they were like sheep without a shepherd. And he began to teach them many things."

Jesus' time had come to shepherd, to lead His people into God's truth. Shepherds lead sheep where they need to go—for good grass to eat, clean water to drink, and a safe place to lie down and rest. In Jesus' time, being a shepherd was a hard job. Sometimes one sheep would get lost and the shepherd would search for it. Sometimes a sheep would get hurt or would keep wandering off. Then, the shepherd would carry it until it was healed and it learned to stay near. Sometimes, a wild animal would steal a sheep from the flock to eat it. The shepherd would risk his life to save that sheep.

Jesus led the crowd's hearts and minds to places where they would have peace. He would teach them how to stay with God. He would heal many of those who needed healing. He would keep His followers close to Him so they would be able to enjoy His presence and His love.

Jesus knew that sin and God's enemies were like wild animals trying to take God's sheep away from the flock. So, Jesus became our shepherd. He fought off the bite and death of the sin threatening to carry us away from God. Jesus, our Good Shepherd, gave up His life on the cross to save us, His sheep.

▙▙ ▙▙ ▙▙

**THIS PSALM SHOWS HOW THE LORD IS OUR SHEPHERD.
PSALM 23**

**HOW ARE PEOPLE LIKE SHEEP AND HOW IS JESUS
LIKE OUR SHEPHERD?**

WHY ARE YOU GLAD THAT JESUS IS THE GOOD SHEPHERD?

Jesus is
The Way, The Truth, and The Life

JESUS SAID TO HIM, "I AM THE WAY, AND THE TRUTH,
AND THE LIFE."
JOHN 14:6A

JESUS IS THE WAY WE GET CLOSE TO GOD AGAIN, THE TRUTH FROM GOD, AND HE PROVIDES FOREVER LIFE WITH GOD.

Hello, Cutie! What is going down, Shorty? Goodbye, Sweetie Pie! Sometimes a nickname tells us something about a person. Jesus gave us some of His names so we could understand more of who He is.

One of Jesus' followers asked how to get to God the Father's house in heaven. "Jesus said to him, 'I am the way, and the truth, and the life. No one comes to the Father except through me.'" Jesus answered a "how?" question with a "who"! Jesus is the answer to more questions than we might realize.

"I Am" is a name for God. When Moses wanted God to tell him His name, God simply said, "I am." When Jesus said "I Am," He was showing that He is God [the Son]. When Jesus said, "I am the way," He was showing that He is the spiritual path to our Father God. The way to God is through believing in Jesus Himself. God will handle the details of how you get to heaven, but the way to be close to God is through believing in Jesus.

In front of funny mirrors you might seem to be super tall, or lumpy, or short, but that is not what you truly look like. Truth is what is real and actual. Jesus is not like a funny mirror. He never lies or gives us the wrong impression. What is real and true is found in Jesus and His teaching in the Bible. Jesus is the only way to God because Jesus is the ultimate Truth.

Spiritually, we are dead without God. When we believe in Jesus, He brings our sin-smothered souls to life. Jesus created all life, and true life is found in Him. Jesus is the true life who brings us close to love and enjoy our Father God. Fake gods, wrong directions, lying ideas or spiritually dead people will never be the way to our Father God. Jesus tells us He is the only way to be close to Father God again, both now and in heaven.

Jesus says, "I am the way, and the truth, and the life. No one comes to the Father except through me."

▰ ▰ ▰

**JESUS ASSURES OTHERS OF WHO HE IS.
JOHN 14:1-6**

HOW IS JESUS THE WAY TO GET TO GOD?

**JESUS IS THE TRUTH, SO HOW MIGHT YOU RESPOND TO SOMEONE
WHO SAID THEY DID NOT BELIEVE JESUS?**

Jesus is a Servant

A SERVANT IS ONE WHO GIVES ATTENTION AND ACTIONS TO THE NEEDS OR DESIRES OF ANOTHER PERSON.

Donkeys clip-clopped, sheep baa-ed, people's voices hummed, and an occasional shout was heard from someone selling provisions to tired travelers. It was the Passover celebration, when all Jews came back to Jerusalem to remember how God saved them in Egypt. There was a special meal and special times at the Temple to remember the night God passed over the Israelites' houses. They remembered how the Israelites were safe under the blood of the lamb while the firstborn son in every Egyptian house died.

This year, Jesus went with His disciples to Jerusalem for the Passover celebration. Jesus had taught, healed, and served for three years. He knew the time was near for Him to die. When they arrived in the city, Jesus and the disciples had to clean themselves up from the journey. Most houses in Jerusalem would have a servant to wash the guests' feet, but this time, someone else would do the job.

Jesus is worthy of our forever praise and worship because He is

God's Son. Jesus created everything. He is the King of kings and Lord of lords, our Deliverer, Savior, High Priest, and the only Way to the Father. Yet, He decided to kneel down, take a towel and water, and wash the grime of animal-filled streets off His followers' feet. Jesus lovingly served the disciples that night, just hours before they would abandon Him.

Jesus chose to be a Servant. He deserved to be honored as the King, yet He stooped down to clean. He served those who were unworthy. After He finished and the bowl was filled with grimy brown water and bits of sand, He washed others' dirt off Himself before sitting down at the table. Then, Jesus explained to His friends what He had just done. He said that even though He was their master and leader, He chose to serve. He said they should serve others as well.

Jesus was not new to serving that Passover night. Jesus served when He stooped down from the glories of heaven to the stench surrounding a manger. Jesus served when He spent His days speaking to sin-plugged ears about the good news of God's kingdom. Jesus served when He spent His weeks healing people filled with disease and sickness. Jesus served when He was nailed to a cross, taking on Himself the disgusting muck of our sin until it killed Him.

Isn't He amazing? Jesus deserves to be served, but before we could ever serve Him, He served us. Jesus became a servant to fulfill God's plan from the very beginning, the plan to bring His people close to Himself again. Jesus, the Holy Servant, "came not to be served but to serve, and to give his life as a ransom for many."

♛ ♛ ♛

THIS IS WHAT JESUS DID AT HIS LAST SUPPER ON EARTH.
JOHN 13:3-5

JESUS WANTS US TO FOLLOW HIS EXAMPLE.
HOW CAN YOU SERVE OTHERS?

IN WHAT WAYS IS JESUS A SERVANT FOR YOU?

43

Jesus is a
Man of Sorrows

**HE WAS DESPISED AND REJECTED BY MEN,
A MAN OF SORROWS AND ACQUAINTED WITH GRIEF.
ISAIAH 53:3A**

**A MAN OF SORROWS IS ONE WHO IS TERRIBLY
SADDENED TO THE POINT OF PAIN IN HIS
THOUGHTS AND BODY.**

Have you ever carried something that was so heavy you nearly dropped it? Maybe you called out for someone to come help you carry the weight? Some things in life are so hard that we cry out for others to come alongside and pray for us. We ask them to carry some of the weight in prayer so we can finish the job God asked us to do.

Jesus is fully God, but He is also fully man. Because He is fully man, He can understand everything we go through. He has felt the pain of carrying things that seem too difficult to bear alone. He understands, and He wants us to cry out for Him to help carry the burden. While He was on earth, Jesus had extremely heavy burdens. There were people always wanting something from Him. He carried the burden of feeling no one on earth could understand Him, of knowing the job He had to do would be terrible to complete.

After the Passover meal where He washed his followers' feet, Jesus and His followers walked to a garden to pray. Jesus felt the burden of all that was about to happen on the cross. He felt this so intensely He was sweating blood! He asked His disciples to pray, but they fell asleep. Jesus was burdened beyond anything we can imagine, but everyone close to Him on earth left Him to carry it alone.

This is what the Bible says happened: "he [Jesus] began to be sorrowful and troubled. Then he said to them, 'My soul is very sorrowful, even to death; remain here, and watch with me.' And going a little farther he fell on his face and prayed, saying, 'My Father, if it be possible, let this cup pass from me; nevertheless, not as I will, but as you will.' And he came to the disciples and found them sleeping."

In many ways, Jesus did not want to endure the cross, but He would do what God the Father desired. Jesus had come to fulfill Their plan from the beginning—to crush the sin that separated people from God.

After the third time Jesus prayed, evil men came to carry Jesus away. They accused Him of doing wrong things He never did. They convinced the Roman government to kill Him for crimes He never committed. Then, Jesus died on a cross for sins He never even attempted.

When we have sorrows, we can know that Jesus understands. When people are punished unfairly, they can know Jesus understands. The sin of the world was a heavy burden. Jesus felt the weight of all that sin, but He carried the weight of sorrow because of joy. It was the joy of doing God the Father's will, the joy of bringing together God and His people again, and the joy of loving His people for all eternity. We can know gladness and joy with God because of our Savior, the Man of Sorrows.

**THIS IS WHAT IT WAS LIKE FOR JESUS.
ISAIAH 53:3-5**

WHEN YOU FEEL SAD, WHAT DO YOU DO?

WHEN WE THINK OF THE CROSS OF JESUS, WE CAN HAVE SO MANY EMOTIONS AT THE SAME TIME. WHAT ARE SOME OF THE EMOTIONS YOU HAVE AND WHY?

Jesus is the Sacrifice for Our Sins

THIS IS LOVE: NOT THAT WE LOVED GOD, BUT THAT HE LOVED US AND SENT HIS SON AS AN ATONING SACRIFICE FOR OUR SINS.
1 JOHN 4:10 (NIV)

THE SACRIFICE FOR OUR SINS IS THE ONE WHO GAVE UP HIS LIFE ON THE CROSS, TAKING THE DEATH WE DESERVED.

Had it only been a few hours since Jesus knelt down to wash the disciples' feet? The Passover celebration was still going strong in Jerusalem. Jesus had come to the city to celebrate what God did thousands of years ago, when the blood of a lamb kept God's people from death. Jesus had celebrated the Passover meal knowing He would soon be the true Lamb of God, who takes away the sin of the world. Now, as His blood stained the wood of the cross, He felt the full weight, pain, and sorrow of sin.

The sign over His head said, "The King of the Jews." Soldiers had put a crown of thorns on His head to make fun of this name. The King of kings and Lord of lords could have caused all the angels of heaven to destroy these evildoers at any second. This Creator, God the Son, could have simply stopped holding together the bodies of

His killers in that moment. Jesus could have gotten down from that cross in the flash of an eye.

But as the high priest sacrificed animals to cover sins at the Temple, Jesus sacrificed Himself not just to cover sins, but to take them on Himself and away from us forever. As Jesus hung by the nails in His hands and feet, He felt the wrath of God the Father towards sin. He did not have to die, but as the Good Shepherd He laid down His life to protect His sheep from the forever deadly fangs of sin.

The soldiers killing Jesus had no idea who He was at first. But then the sky went black for hours in the middle of the day, and the ground below their feet trembled and shook the moment Jesus died. Then, one of the soldiers spoke, "Truly this was the Son of God!"

Do you remember when we read about the Temple and the Holy of Holies? There was a thick curtain there to separate God's dwelling place in the Holy of Holies from the people. The second Jesus died, the curtain ripped down the middle from top to bottom. No man could have reached the top of it, except the One higher and holier than any created person—God the Father.

That rip was really a mend, a bringing back together. It looked like a tear, but it was a repair of the relationship between God the Father and those who belong to Him through faith. Sin no longer separated God from His beloved children.

Jesus is the way to God the Father, and God the Father made that clear! He is the way because He is the sacrifice for our sin. Thank you, Jesus.

♦ ♦ ♦

**WHEN JESUS DIED A LOT OF THINGS HAPPENED.
MATTHEW 27:50-51**

WHY IS JESUS DYING ON THE CROSS SUCH A BIG DEAL?

**THE CURTAIN OF THE HOLY OF HOLIES RIPPED.
WHY IS THAT IMPORTANT?**

Jesus is the Resurrection and the Life

JESUS SAID TO HER, "I AM THE RESURRECTION AND THE LIFE. WHOEVER BELIEVES IN ME, THOUGH HE DIE, YET SHALL HE LIVE."
JOHN 11:25

THE RESURRECTION IS THE ONE WHO CAN BRING BACK TO LIFE BOTH BODY AND SOUL. THE LIFE IS THE ONE WHO PROVIDES THE FULLNESS OF ABUNDANT LIFE BOTH NOW AND FOREVER IN ETERNITY.

In the days following Jesus' death, the dark shadow of the cross made the light of hope seem dim. Jesus' friends huddled together behind locked doors. They were afraid they might be the next ones crucified.

After Jesus died, His body was wrapped in clean cloths, much like He had been wrapped as a baby. But instead of being placed in a manger, He was placed in a tomb. This tomb was a small cave, and its opening was covered by a huge stone.

Once the stone was rolled in front of the opening, Roman soldiers came to guard the tomb. It was odd to see soldiers guarding a dead body, but they were there because Jesus' enemies, the religious leaders, were concerned. The religious leaders knew Jesus had said things about being raised up in three days. They wanted to make sure Jesus stayed in the tomb. But God will never be controlled by people.

On Sunday morning, the third day after Jesus died, some of His followers walked to the tomb. They were sad and confused. But in a moment, their eyes widened with shock and their bodies froze with fear. What did they see? That huge stone was rolled away from the tomb entrance and sitting on top of that stone was an angel, gleaming with light! He kindly explained, "Do not be afraid, for I know that you seek Jesus who was crucified. He is not here, for He has risen, as He said."

The next moment, the followers saw the most amazing thing human eyes have ever seen: the resurrected Jesus. He had come back to life! They stopped feeling sad and afraid that instant. Rushing rivers of hope filled their hearts to overflowing!

Over the next 40 days, Jesus appeared to around 500 of His followers. He ate with them, talked with them, and taught them. Seeing the resurrected Jesus filled them with awe in their hearts that turned to faith in their souls. Jesus' close followers were surer of God than ever. Jesus being alive changed them because it changed everything. They had no doubt that Jesus is God the Son, because only God has power over death. Only the Creator of life can overcome death.

The men who ran away when Jesus was crucified now stood strong in their faith. Instead of hiding behind locked doors, the disciples were ready to help spread the good news of God's kingdom. Jesus' resurrection gave them faith. They had faith that Jesus would give them forever life in heaven. Even though our bodies may die, people who believe in Jesus will be resurrected like Jesus to have a forever life in heaven. Jesus is our Resurrection and our Life.

ﯓ ﯓ ﯓ

JESUS DID NOT JUST DIE AND REMAIN DEAD.
1 CORINTHIANS 15:3-4

HOW DOES JESUS' RESURRECTION GIVE YOU CONFIDENCE?

WHY IS JESUS CALLED OUR RESURRECTION AND OUR LIFE?

Jesus is the Head of the Church

**AND HE [JESUS] IS THE HEAD OF
THE BODY, THE CHURCH.
COLOSSIANS 1:18A**

**THE HEAD OF THE CHURCH IS THE ONE WHO IS THE
LEADER AND LORD OF THE CHURCH.**

Have you ever been on a team that worked well together? What about a team that did not work well together? One thing that makes a team work well is agreeing who is the leader, then others follow what the leader says. When the leader is doing a good job, the team does too.

All people who believe in Jesus are called "His church." Sometimes they are called "the body," because people who believe in Jesus should work like a team the way your body works together to run or climb or draw. How does a body know what to do? Your brain in your head is the leader of your body, just like Jesus is the leader of all His believers (the church). The church needs to follow what the leader says. If they all listen and work together, great things happen!

The Bible says Jesus is the head, the leader, of the church. After spending 40 days with His followers, He went up to heaven to sit on His forever throne next to God the Father. Before

He ascended, He gave the church these directions: "Go therefore and make disciples of all nations, baptizing them in the name of the Father and of the Son and of the Holy Spirit, teaching them to observe all that I have commanded you. And behold, I am with you always, to the end of the age."

These directions are sometimes called the "Great Commission." Remember how God promised Abraham that through him all the families of the earth would be blessed? God keeps this promise through the Great Commission. As Jesus' followers tell people all over the earth about Him, God changes their hearts. When people believe in Jesus, Abraham's great-grandson, God brings them close to Himself again.

Jesus has given every person who believes in Him special ways they can help the church, the body of Christ, follow the Great Commission. Each believer gets their own part of this important job.

On our own, the Great Commission is actually an impossible mission. We cannot do anything by ourselves to change the hearts of other people. But Jesus has given us a Helper who has the power to do that!

Jesus gave us His Holy Spirit, who is God, to be with us all the time. When we obey the Great Commission, the Holy Spirit gives us words to tell about Jesus and the courage to say them. The Holy Spirit also opens people's hearts and minds so they understand Jesus and believe in Him. In all of this, Jesus is the leader, the director, and the Head of the Church.

⩊ ⩊ ⩊

**JESUS SENDS HIS DISCIPLES OUT AND PROMISES TO BE WITH THEM.
MATTHEW 25:18-20**

**WHAT SPECIAL MISSION (OR GREAT COMMISSION)
DID JESUS GIVE HIS FOLLOWERS?**

**HOW CAN YOU OR YOUR FAMILY OBEY
THE GREAT COMMISSION IN DAY-TO-DAY LIFE?**

Jesus is our Advocate

BUT IF ANYONE DOES SIN, WE HAVE AN ADVOCATE WITH THE FATHER, JESUS CHRIST THE RIGHTEOUS.
1 JOHN 2:1B

AN ADVOCATE IS ONE WHO WILL COME ALONGSIDE YOU TO COMFORT, HELP, AND DEFEND YOU.

Has someone ever stood up for you when you were in trouble? We call the one who does this your advocate. When a person believes in Jesus, old sin thoughts sometimes lure us into trouble again. When we do share our belief in Jesus with others, sometimes we get into trouble with unbelievers. Jesus is the Advocate who speaks to God the Father for us. With Jesus as our Advocate, we are forgiven by God because Jesus lived the perfect life for us and died for us. With Jesus as our Advocate, we are empowered by God to obey even when it is hard.

Jesus sits right beside God the Father in heaven. Because He is close to God and close to us, Jesus is the perfect Advocate. Even though we cannot see Jesus, He is always watching us from His throne. When Jesus sees that one of his followers needs help, He will be their Advocate to ask God the Father.

After Jesus returned to heaven, His followers began to obey His Great Commission. One of these followers was named Stephen. The Holy Spirit gave him power to do miracles and teach about Jesus in a way that demanded attention. Before long, the same religious leaders who had killed Jesus wanted to get Stephen in trouble, too. They asked him to explain himself.

Stephen began telling the stories of Abraham, Joseph, Moses and even King David. At first, the religious leaders nodded their heads in agreement. They thought he was proving that they were right. They did not know these old stories were part of God the Father's bigger plan to send Jesus. But then Stephen explained how those stories told of the Messiah's coming.

The leaders stopped nodding their heads now. Their necks stiffened with anger. When Stephen accused them of ignoring the Messiah, bullying him and killing Him, the leaders were "enraged, and they ground their teeth at him. But he [Stephen], full of the Holy Spirit, gazed into heaven and saw the glory of God, and Jesus standing at the right hand of God."

Stephen could not believe what he saw! Jesus, the Advocate, was there, knew everything, and was standing up for Stephen! Jesus knew Stephen was about to be killed, so Jesus stood up for him in the way only God the Son can. He filled Stephen with the Holy Spirit, who gave Stephen peace—even as the leaders threw rocks at him until he died.

God may allow things to happen that seem bad, but Jesus will be right there helping as our Advocate. God takes all bad things that come to Jesus' followers and uses them for good. After Stephen died, many people heard his story and believed in Jesus because of it. God may allow bad things to come and you will still sin, but Jesus is watching and standing up for those who believe in Him. We will never be alone or helpless with Jesus as our Advocate.

▂▂ ▂▂ ▂▂

HERE, JESUS STANDS UP FOR STEPHEN.
ACTS 7:54-57

HOW DOES JESUS STAND UP FOR HIS BELIEVERS?

WHY IS JESUS OUR PERFECT ADVOCATE?

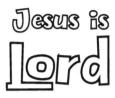

Jesus is Lord

**"SURELY I AM COMING SOON." AMEN.
COME, LORD JESUS!
REVELATION 22:20B**

THE LORD IS THE MASTER WHO HAS THE POWER AND AUTHORITY OVER HIS PEOPLE'S LIVES.

Who has the right to tell you what to do? How do you feel when someone has power over you? Most people wish no one told them what to do.

Jesus is Lord, which means He is the powerful leader of His creation and is in control of everything. When we believe in Jesus, knowing that He is Lord makes us joyful. Knowing He is in control makes us feel "Garden of Eden" freedom and happiness. Our respect and wonder at His power bubbles up in our hearts into a faith that is sure of Jesus.

Can you imagine being glad someone can tell you what to do? Anyone who believes in Jesus is happy to let Jesus lead them! When Jesus is someone's Lord, that person listens to Him, trusts Him, and obeys Him.

Right now, Jesus is calling people to follow Him as Lord, but people think they know best for themselves. They do not want to admit that Jesus is their Creator and a Creator knows how His creation works best. They do not want to admit that Jesus is the Way, the Truth, and the Life. Jesus de-

54

serves obedience, faithfulness, respect, and love, but He does not demand it—yet.

At Christmas, everyone remembers Jesus' first coming as a baby in Bethlehem, but this isn't the only good news to remember. Jesus is not just coming to the earth once. Jesus is coming a second time to make all things right and new and perfect, once and for all. When Jesus comes again, He will bring everyone who loves Him to heaven, where they will get to join a huge celebration! They will rejoice because Jesus finished God's plan to bring His people close again!

Jesus will then make everything right so His followers never again experience sin, pain, loss, shame, or death. Everyone who has ever lived will "bow, in heaven and on earth and under the earth, and every tongue confess that Jesus Christ is Lord, to the glory of God the Father." Sadly, those who now refuse to admit Jesus is Lord will then be sent away from God forever, which is the worst punishment imaginable.

Now, every person is called to either admit Jesus is their Lord or ignore Jesus and be sent away from God forever. How is someone saved from forever separation from God? "If you confess with your mouth that Jesus is Lord and believe in your heart that God raised him from the dead, you will be saved."

I hope you have said "Jesus is Lord," and that you believe it and it makes you happy! I hope you are sure of God and sure that God raised Jesus from the dead. If you believe this of Jesus, then you are a follower of Jesus who will be forever with God. If you do not believe Jesus is Lord, why not? Talk to a family member or pastor who is a Jesus follower about your thoughts. Jesus is Lord whether we admit it now or later. I hope and pray you can now admit and believe that Jesus is your Lord.

♛ ♛ ♛

JESUS TELLS US HE IS COMING BACK.
REVELATION 22:20-21

WHAT DOES IT MEAN WHEN SOMEONE SAYS JESUS IS THEIR LORD?

WHAT IN YOUR LIFE SHOWS THAT JESUS IS YOUR LORD?

Scripture References

Introduction

Hear, O Israel: The Lord our God, the Lord is one. Deuteronomy 6:4

Jesus is the Creator

And God said, "Let there be light," and there was light. Genesis 1:3 (ESV)

For by him all things were created, in heaven and on earth, visible and invisible, whether thrones or dominions or rulers or authorities—all things were created through him and for him. Colossians 1:16

And he is before all things, and in him all things hold together. Colossians 1:17

Jesus is the Savior

I will put enmity between you and the woman, and between your offspring and her offspring; he shall bruise your head, and you shall bruise his heel. Genesis 3:15

Jesus is the Author and Perfecter of Faith

I will bless those who bless you, and him who dishonors you I will curse, and in you all the families of the earth shall be blessed. Genesis 12:3

Jesus is the Deliverer

Genesis 12:3

Jesus is the Lamb of God

Then the Lord said to Moses, "Go in to Pharaoh and say to him, 'Thus says the Lord, the God of the Hebrews, "Let my people go, that they may serve me." Exodus 9:1

So the heart of Pharaoh was hardened, and he did not let the people of Israel go, just as the Lord had spoken through Moses. Exodus 9:35

Jesus is the One Who Sets Us Free

And Moses said to the people, "Fear not, stand firm, and see the salvation of the Lord, which he will work for you today. For the Egyptians whom you see today, you shall never see again. The Lord will fight for you, and you have only to be silent." Exodus 14:13-14

Bread of Life

When the people of Israel saw it, they said to one another, "What is it?" For they did not know what it was. And Moses said to them, "It is the bread that the Lord has given you to eat." Exodus 16:15

Jesus is the King of kings and Lord of lords

And the Lord said to Samuel, "Obey the voice of the people in all that they say to you, for they have not rejected you, but they have rejected me from being king over them." 1 Samuel 8:7

On his robe and on his thigh he has a name written, King of kings and Lord of lords. Revelation 19:16

Therefore God has highly exalted him and bestowed on him the name that is above every name, so that at the name of Jesus every knee should bow, in heaven and on earth and under the earth, and every tongue confess that Jesus Christ is Lord, to the glory of God the Father. Philippians 2:9-11

Jesus is the Son of David

And your house and your kingdom shall be made sure forever before me. Your throne shall be established forever. 2 Samuel 7:16

Jesus is the Messiah

But you, O Bethlehem Ephrathah, who are too little to be among the clans of Judah, from you shall come forth for me one who is to be ruler in Israel, whose coming forth is from of old, from ancient days. Micah 5:2

Jesus is the Wonderful Counselor, Mighty God, Everlasting Father, Prince of Peace

For to us a child is born, to us a son is given; and the government shall be upon his shoulder, and his name shall be called Wonderful Counselor, Mighty God, Everlasting Father, Prince of Peace. Isaiah 9:6

For God so loved the world, that He gave His only begotten Son, that whoever believes in Him shall not perish, but have eternal life. John 3:16 (NASB)

Jesus is Immanuel

"Behold, the virgin shall conceive and bear a son, and they shall call his name Immanuel" (which means, God with us). Matthew 1:23

Jesus is The Christ

And the angel said to them, "Fear not, for behold, I bring you good news of great joy that will be for all the people. For unto you is born this day in the city of David a Savior, who is Christ the Lord." Luke 2:10-11

Jesus is the Good Shepard

When he went ashore he saw a great crowd, and he had compassion on them, because they were like sheep without a shepherd. And he began to teach them many things. Mark 6:34

Jesus is The Way, The Truth, and The Life

Jesus said to him, "I am the way, and the truth, and the life. No one comes to the Father except through me." John 14:6

Jesus is a Servant

Even as the Son of Man came not to be served but to serve, and to give his life as a ransom for many. Matthew 20:28

Jesus is a Man of Sorrows

Then he said to them, "My soul is very sorrowful, even to death; remain here, and watch with me." And going a little farther he fell on his face and prayed, saying, "My Father, if it be possible, let this cup pass from me; nevertheless, not as I will, but as you will." And he came to the disciples and found them sleeping. Matthew 26:38-40A

Jesus is the Sacrifice for Our Sins

And over his head they put the charge against him, which read, "This is Jesus, the King of the Jews." Matthew 27:37

When the centurion and those who were with him, keeping watch over Jesus, saw the earthquake and what took place, they were filled with awe and said, "Truly this was the Son of God!" Matthew 27:54

Jesus is the Resurrection and the Life

But the angel said to the women, "Do not be afraid, for I know that you seek Jesus who was crucified. He is not here, for he has risen, as he said. Come, see the place where he lay." Matthew 28:5-6

Jesus is the Head of the Church

Go therefore and make disciples of all nations, baptizing them in the name of the Father and of the Son and of the Holy Spirit, teaching them to observe all that I have commanded you. And behold, I am with you always, to the end of the age. Matthew 28:19-20

Jesus is our Advocate

Now when they heard these things they were enraged, and they ground their teeth at him. But he, full of the Holy Spirit, gazed into heaven and saw the glory of God, and Jesus standing at the right hand of God. Acts 7:54-55

Jesus is Lord

So that at the name of Jesus every knee should bow, in heaven and on earth and under the earth, and every tongue confess that Jesus Christ is Lord, to the glory of God the Father. Philippians 2:10-11

Because, if you confess with your mouth that Jesus is Lord and believe in your heart that God raised him from the dead, you will be saved. Romans 10:9